★ IT'S MY STATE! ★

ALABAMA

Joyce Hart

Cavendish
Square
New York

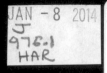
Published in 2014 by Cavendish Square Publishing, LLC
303 Park Avenue South, Suite 1247, New York, NY 10010

Copyright © 2014 by Cavendish Square Publishing, LLC

Second Edition

Website: cavendishsq.com

This publication represents the opinions and views of the authors based on their personal experience, knowledge, and research. The information in this book serves as a general guide only. The authors and publisher have used their best efforts in preparing this book and disclaim liability rising directly or indirectly from the use and application of this book.

CPSIA Compliance Information: Batch #WW14CSQ

All websites were available and accurate when this book was sent to press.

Library of Congress Cataloging-in-Publication Data

Hart, Joyce, 1954-
Alabama / Joyce Hart.
    pages cm. — (It's my state)
Includes index.
ISBN 978-1-62712-221-4 (hardcover) ISBN 978-1-62712-477-5 (paperback) ISBN 978-1-62712-232-0 (ebook)
1. Alabama—Juvenile literature. I. Title.

F326.3.H372 2014
976.1—dc23

                    2013032176

This edition developed for Cavendish Square Publishing by RJF Publishing LLC (www.RJFpublishing.com)
Series Designer, Second Edition: Tammy West/Westgraphix LLC
Editorial Director: Dean Miller
Editor: Sara Howell
Copy Editor: Cynthia Roby
Art Director: Jeffrey Talbot
Layout Design: Erica Clendening
Production Manager: Jennifer Ryder-Talbot

All maps, illustrations, and graphics © Cavendish Square Publishing, LLC. Maps and artwork on pages 6, 26, 27, 75, 76, and back cover by Christopher Santoro. Map and graphics on pages 8 and 46 by Westgraphix LLC.

The photographs in this book are used by permission and through the courtesy of: Cover (main), cover (inset), p. 5 (bottom), pp. 8, 13, 14, 15, 18, 52, 56, 57, 67, 73 (bottom) Shutterstock.com; p. 4 (top) Photo Researchers, Inc.: David Hosking; p. 4 (bottom) Animals Animals: Maresa Pryor; pp. 5 (top), 50 (top), 53 Wikimedia Commons; pp. 9, 46 Raymond Gehman; pp. 10, 62 Richard Cummins; p. 11, 58 Prisma; p. 16 Kevin Fleming; pp. 17, 44 Buddy Mays; p. 19 (top) Stephen J. Krasemann; p. 19 (bottom) Michael P. Gadomski; pp. 20, 35, 36 Corbis; p. 23 Richard A. Cooke; pp. 24, 26 De Agostini Picture Library/Getty Images; pp. 25, 29, 33, 34 Northwind Pictures; p. 27 David David Gallery; p. 37 SuperStock; p. 38 Bettmann; pp. 39, 55 Flip Schulke; p. 41 Warren Faidley; p. 42 Richard T. Nowitz; p. 48 Charles Rotkin; p. 49 Gary S. Chapman/Getty Images; p. 50 (bottom) Reuters; p. 51 (top) Northfoto/Getty Images; p. 51 (bottom) Associated Press: Robert Sutton; p. 54 The Image Works: Jeff Greenberg; p. 64 Lowell Georgia; p. 68 U.S. Department of Agriculture; p. 69 Bill Varie; p. 70 Greg Smith; p. 72 M.E. Warren; p. 73 (top) Philip Gould.

Every effort has been made to locate the copyright holders of the images used in this book.

Printed in the United States of America.

CONTENTS

State Wildflower: Oakleaf Hydrangea

The oakleaf hydrangea was confirmed as Alabama's official state wildflower in 1999. It is native to all 67 counties of the state. Naturalist William Bartram discovered the oakleaf hydrangea as he traveled through the area between 1775 and 1776. The oakleaf hydrangea, which can grow to 6 feet (1.8 m) tall, produces beautiful white blooms in the summer.

State Bird: Yellowhammer

One of the unofficial nicknames of Alabama comes from this small bird. The yellowhammer is also called a flicker and is a member of the woodpecker family. The male yellowhammers have yellow feathers in their wings. Both males and females have sharp claws to help them cling to the sides of the tree trunks.

State Tree: Southern Longleaf Pine

Officially named as the state tree in 1997, the southern longleaf pine grows in forests throughout the southern portions of Alabama. This pine tree has 12-inch-(30.5 cm) long needles that grow in clusters of three.

State Animal:
Alabama Red-Bellied Turtle

The Alabama red-bellied turtle is native to Alabama and lives in either fresh or brackish (somewhat salty) water in the Mobile Delta and in the waters of Baldwin County. One of the most interesting things about this turtle is that in the wild it only lives in Alabama. The Alabama red-bellied turtle was placed on the U. S. Fish and Wildlife Service's Endangered Species List in 1987.

State Nut: Pecan

Pecan trees thrive in Alabama, so it comes as no surprise that the pecan was named the state nut in 1982. The pecan nut grows inside a thin, oval shell that is easy to crack. The sweet nut is a popular snack and is used in many Southern recipes.

State Rock: Marble

Alabama is known around the world for its marble, a rock that is made up of the recrystallized minerals limestone or dolomite. Marble comes in a variety of colors such as pink, red, gray, and black. Most of Alabama's marble is found in Talladega County from the Coosa River southward. In the past, Alabama's marble was used in making monuments and buildings. Today it is also ground up and used in such products as soil conditioners, paints, and plastics. Marble was made the state rock in 1969.

ALABAMA

Florence
Tennessee River
U.S. Rocket Center & Space Camp
Huntsville

Sipsey River

Anniston

Birmingham
Coosa River

Tuscaloosa

Demopolis

Selma

Montgomery

Auburn

Chattahoochee River

Eufaula

Tombigbee River

Alabama River

Jackson

Conecuh River

Pea River

Enterprise

Dothan

Mobile River
Tensaw River

Mobile

Mississippi Sound

GULF OF MEXICO

N
W   E
S

The Heart of Dixie

Alabama is located in the southeastern part of the United States. Its geography varies from forested mountains in the north to sandy beaches along the Gulf of Mexico in the south. With its gentle climate and friendly people, Alabama is a great place to live.

Alabama covers more than 52,000 square miles (134,679 sq. km), making it the thirtieth-largest state. Alabama is almost rectangular in shape, measuring about 300 miles (483 km) north to south and about 200 miles (322 km) east to west. The land surface of the southern portion of the state is made up of low hills and flat valleys. As you travel from Mobile in the southwest to the Appalachian Mountains in the northeast, the elevation of the land slowly rises, changing from sea level to almost 2,000 feet (610 m). If you completed a tour of the entire state, you would see everything from sandy shorelines to fertile valleys, broad prairies, swampy bogs, limestone caves, evergreen forests, and rocky mountainsides. Scientists have studied these features and have divided Alabama into six different regions, each with its own distinctive traits.

Quick Facts

Alabama's Borders

North	Tennessee
South	Florida
	Gulf of Mexico
East	Georgia
West	Mississippi

The East Gulf Coastal Plain

The largest region is the East Gulf Coastal Plain, which covers most of the southern and western parts of Alabama. In the southern part of this plain is the Mobile River Delta, where swamplands drain into the Gulf of Mexico. Also found here is Alabama's major seaport.

In the northern part of the plain, which stretches almost to Tennessee, the land is creased with rows of hills that run in an east-to-west pattern. You will find farmlands and forests in this area. Farther east on the plain, cows, pigs, and poultry are raised. Peanut crops are also grown in the region. Large cities in this area include Mobile in the far south, Montgomery in the central portion, and Tuscaloosa farther north.

In the middle of the East Gulf Coastal Plain is the Black Belt, which runs along the Alabama River Valley. This strip of prairie land almost cuts the state in two, dividing northern and southern Alabama. This region got its name because of its black, sticky soil, which was, at one time, a great place to grow cotton. Today, farmers here mostly raise livestock. Selma is the region's major city.

Mobile Bay is an estuary, or area where the ocean meets a river.

Rock climbers stare down from a granite cliff in Cheaha State Park. The cliffs are near Mount Cheaha—sometimes called Cheaha Mountain—the state's highest point.

The Piedmont Plateau

Northeast of the Black Belt region is the Piedmont Plateau. The highest point in Alabama, Mount Cheaha, which stretches to 2,408 feet (734 m), is located here in Lineville. Also found in the Piedmont Plateau are Alabama's famous marble quarries and other rock and mineral deposits, such as coal, iron, and limestone. The Piedmont Plateau is an area of hills, ridges, and valleys.

The Appalachian Ridge and Valley Region

Just north of the Piedmont is the Appalachian Ridge and Valley Region where more deposits of coal, iron ore, and limestone are found. These minerals make up the ingredients for steel, which is produced in Alabama's steel mills. The southernmost tip of the Appalachian Mountains is located in this region. The Appalachian Mountains are a chain of mountains that run from Alabama to Maine.

The Cumberland Plateau

The Cumberland Plateau lies in the northeastern corner of Alabama. A plateau is an area of high ground that is level, such as a flat-top mountain. Although the land in this area is relatively flat, in some places it still rises to about 1,800 feet (549 m).

The bodies of water in this area, such as Guntersville Lake, support almost one hundred different types of fish. There are many caves here, too, which are great habitats for different varieties of bats. Two of Alabama's most famous caves are Cathedral and Rickwood Caverns.

Located in north-central Alabama, Birmingham has the highest population in the state.

Many Alabama residents and visitors enjoy exploring the state's caves and caverns.

The Interior Low Plateau

The Interior Low Plateau lies in the northernmost part of the state. There the land is made up mostly of limestone, which is a whitish-colored rock usually made from the remains of ancient sea creatures. Fed by the Tennessee River, the fertile valleys in this section are ideal for farmers. Farms and ranches in the region raise cattle and other livestock and grow crops such as corn and cotton. Huntsville and Decatur are the biggest Alabama cities in this area.

The Waterways

Alabama has more than 900 square miles (2,331 sq. km) of rivers and artificial, or manmade, lakes. There are 26 rivers in Alabama. The longest rivers are the Tombigbee River, which is 400 miles (644 km) long, and the Alabama River, which is 300 miles (483 km) long. Most of Alabama's major rivers run in a north-to-south direction and drain into the Gulf of Mexico. The one exception is the Tennessee River, which runs east to west. The Mobile, Alabama, and Tombigbee rivers are three of the most important rivers in the state. The Alabama River flows from Montgomery and meets the Tombigbee to form the Mobile River just north of the city of Mobile.

There are no large naturally occurring lakes in Alabama. However, manmade dams on some of the state's rivers have created artificial lakes, such as Guntersville Lake on the Tennessee River. Damming of the Coosa River has formed Weiss, Lay, Mitchell, Jordan, and Logan Martin lakes.

At the southwestern tip of the state you can enjoy the warm waters of the Gulf of Mexico. Alabama's only outlet to the Gulf of Mexico is along Mobile Bay. The state's coastline along the Gulf is about 50 miles (80 km) long. When you add the coastlines that occur along Mobile Bay and other smaller inlets in the area, though, Alabama's shoreline measures more than 600 miles (966 km).

Over the years, Alabama's beaches have been affected by erosion, which is the wearing away of land by wind and waves. In 2010 an offshore oil rig in the Gulf of Mexico exploded and sank. For almost three months, oil gushed into the Gulf, affecting Alabama's beaches and marine life.

The Climate

Alabamians enjoy a subtropical climate, which means they experience short, mild winters and long, warm summers. In winter, the average high temperature ranges between about 45°F (7.2°C) and 55°F (12.7°C), depending on the elevation of the land. People living at higher elevations will have cooler weather than those living closer to sea level. During the summer, temperatures are usually closer to 85°F (29.4°C). Very low or very high temperatures are unusual. The highest temperature ever recorded in Alabama was 112°F (44.4°C) on September 5, 1925, in Centreville. The record low temperature was -27°F (-32.7°C) at New Market on January 30, 1966.

Thunderstorms are common in Alabama, especially in the southern parts of the state, where the warm air from the Gulf of Mexico mixes with the cooler air from the north. In the summer, Alabamians see a lot of rain, which ranges from 53 to 68 inches (135–173 cm) each year. Large storms, such as hurricanes and tornadoes, sometimes cross Alabama, causing flooding and very strong winds.

After the 2010 oil spill, oil washed up on many Gulf beaches, like this one in Gulf Shores.

Sometimes snow falls in the winter, but usually only in the northern mountains. In March 1993, a storm crossed the state, causing a surprising 24 inches (61 cm) of snow to fall all over northern Alabama.

Wildlife

Alabama is home to a large number of different plants. Some of the most common trees include oak, hickory, magnolia, elm, ash, pine, and maple. There are trees that produce flowers, trees that are used for lumber, and trees that produce food. The most popular trees that bear nuts include the pecan and the black walnut. There are also trees that have medicinal use and are used to make people feel better. Sassafras is one example. Native Americans in the region made teas and liquid medicines from the roots of the tree.

Many different flowers grow in the state, but Alabama is most famous for its variety of azaleas. There are also several varieties of wildflowers, which you may see growing along the roadsides, in the prairies and mountains, and even in the backyards of many Alabamians.

Oakleaf hydrangea is native to the southeastern United States. It is often grown in gardens.

Azaleas are famous for their beautiful flowers. The leaves and nectar of azalea plants are highly toxic, though.

Because Alabama has a lot of undisturbed or undeveloped land, there are many wild animals in the state. Raccoons, foxes, squirrels, deer, and rabbits can be found in Alabama's forests. There are also many larger animals, such as bobcats and bears. Beavers make their homes near Alabama's waterways.

Alabama's rivers, lakes, and streams are home to a variety of freshwater fish. These include bass, sunfish, pikes, eels, catfish, and perch. All of these fish provide food for Alabama's large wildlife, but they also attract human fishermen. It is not uncommon to see fishermen casting their lines in the early morning or early evening.

The state's coastal waters are also filled with aquatic life. Red snapper and grouper are types of fish that live on the coastal reefs. Other sea creatures, such as crabs, oysters, and shrimp, thrive in the Gulf's salty waters.

Many birds make their homes in Alabama. Some live there throughout the year, while others migrate to Alabama to stay warm during the winter. Birds in the Heart of Dixie include cardinals, wrens, bluebirds, martins, hummingbirds,

White egrets wade in Alabama's marshes.

eagles, and hawks. Waterbirds such as ducks, loons, and herons can be found in or around the state's lakes and rivers. On the coast, Alabamians may see pelicans and cormorants. Because of the variety of birds in the state, Alabama is a favorite place for birdwatchers.

Protecting Alabama

As in other states, Alabama has many endangered and threatened plants and animals. Wildlife becomes threatened or endangered when habitats are lost, mostly through human interference such as cutting down forests or using land for buildings. Pollution also affects wild animal populations, either by directly hurting the animals or hurting the food the animals eat. Government officials, scientists, and regular Alabama citizens are working hard to keep these animals from becoming extinct, or completely disappearing.

One example of an endangered species in Alabama is the gray bat. Gray bats live in caves throughout Alabama, with the largest populations found in the northern part of the state. The bats choose caves that are close to rivers or lakes

An American alligator rests near a lake in Eufaula. Alabamians are trying to find ways to live peacefully with all of the state's native wildlife, before more plants and animals become endangered.

because their diet is made up of insects that live on or near water. Cutting down trees around caves takes away the protective covering that gray bats need to fly safely to and from the water. In recent years, the loss of habitat has caused gray bats to be put on the Endangered Species list.

In the past, Alabama was not known for its environmental protection programs, but that has changed. Over time, Alabamians have become more informed about keeping the state's water clean and protecting all the wild creatures—right down to the tiny beach mouse. Around the state, many organizations have been established to keep the natural beauty of Alabama alive. Groups of volunteers have come together to protect the state's wildflowers, the great rivers, the lush forests, and the coastal beaches. Alabamians are working hard. They know they live in a wonderful state, and they want to keep it that way.

Plants & Animals

Wild Turkey

At one time, the number of wild turkeys living in Alabama was very low. But Alabamians have worked to bring this large bird back. Wild turkeys are one of the biggest birds in North America and can grow to be 4 feet (1.2 m) long from head to tail. Even though the wild turkey is big, it is a fast flier, especially over short distances. It can sometimes go as fast as 55 miles per hour (89 km/h).

Monarch Butterfly

While the eastern tiger swallowtail holds the title of Alabama's state butterfly, the monarch butterfly is the state's official insect. Monarch butterflies are easily recognized by their bright orange, black, and white wings. Monarchs lay their eggs on milkweed plants, which are found throughout the state.

White-Tailed Deer

White-tailed deer are found all over Alabama, even in or near major cities. When the deer are young fawns, they have white spots on their sides. This helps them hide from danger. As they grow, the spots disappear and their coats are mostly brown. The deer's keen sense of smell and its sharp sense of hearing help to keep it out of danger.

Black Bear

The black bear is the official state mammal of Alabama. It is uncertain how many wild black bears still live in Alabama, though. Scientists have seen bears in some of the swamplands, but they are not yet sure if the bears live there or are just passing through. Black bears usually stand between 4 and 7 feet (1.2-2.1 m) tall. Adult males can weigh as much as 500 pounds (227 kg). Black bears eat plants, berries, nuts, fruits, and insects.

Poison Ivy

Poison ivy is found throughout much of North America. In Alabama, the plant's berries are the yellowhammer's favorite food. Humans should try to stay away from poison ivy because the plant's oils, which are found all over it, can cause painful and very itchy skin problems. Poison ivy can be identified by its glossy three-leafed form

Goldenrod

At one time goldenrod was the state flower of Alabama. It is a very common wildflower with many different varieties. All goldenrod plants have long spikes of bright yellow flowers. Goldenrods attract butterflies, and many Alabamians plant the flowers in their gardens to attract these pretty insects.

From the Beginning

The First Residents

The first people to live in the land now called Alabama are often called Paleo-Indians. Scientists have estimated these early inhabitants may have lived here as many as 9,000 years ago. It is believed they originally came from Asia to North America across a land bridge between the two continents that no longer exists.

Paleo-Indians may have first reached the region that includes Alabama around 7000 BC. They made homes in the many limestone caves here. The caves sheltered them from the rain and the cold in winter and kept them cool in summer. The thick forests and clear rivers provided them with food. They hunted bear and deer, gathered nuts and fruits, and caught fish and turtles.

Several thousand years later, the native people living in the region built large mounds. Scientists and historians today often call these people Mound Builders. Some native groups built homes on top of the mounds. Other groups built religious temples or used the mounds as sacred burial places. Then, about six hundred years later, the Mound Builders disappeared. No one knows for sure what happened to them. They may have been killed by a deadly disease.

In the early 1920s, Alabama children often worked to help support their families.

It is also possible that they ran out of food and moved to another region. Today some of the mounds remain in many states. In Alabama mounds still exist in Hale County, Baldwin County, and on Dauphin Island.

The Creek Confederacy

Many years after the Mound Builders disappeared, new groups of native people began living in the region. Although these bands of natives each had their own names, the British later referred to them as Creeks. This was because the natives built their villages on the banks of creeks, or small branches of larger rivers.

When Europeans arrived in the Creeks' land, the Creeks formed a larger group, called the Creek Confederacy, to protect themselves. The Confederacy was made up of more than seventeen different native groups that spoke the same language, which was called Muskogean.

The Creeks were farmers. They grew corn, beans, and squash and raised cows, pigs, and horses. They lived in well-organized villages. Each community had its own leaders who met every day to discuss problems and solutions.

Although the Creeks fought with the earliest European explorers, they learned to trust later settlers and even offered food to prevent these Europeans from starving. The Creeks were very generous. They welcomed strangers to their villages and eventually adjusted to many of the European customs. Many Creeks even married Europeans.

Visitors to the state can see what is left of the early natives' mounds at Moundville Park.

This painting by William Henry Powell shows Hernando de Soto discovering the Mississippi River.

The Spanish Explorers

The coastline of present-day Alabama was explored by Europeans early in the sixteenth century, but no one is certain of the exact date. Historians do know, however, that the outline of Mobile Bay first appeared on a map of North America in 1505. It was not until 1519 that an official visit was recorded, though. Spain's Alonso Álvarez de Pineda sailed into Mobile Bay but did not stay there very long.

In 1539, Hernando de Soto, the governor of Cuba, landed in what is now Tampa Bay, Florida. He had with him a well-armed group of about 700 men. First, de Soto marched his men to what is now Tennessee, and then turned south and entered the area of present-day Alabama. De Soto was looking for gold. When he could not find it, he went into native American villages, forced his way into their homes, and stole anything of value. De Soto and his men also often beat and tortured the native people if they did not follow his orders. His men also stole their food and horses. Word of Hernando de Soto's bad reputation

Some of the Native American villages that de Soto visited may have looked like this one, which was located near Malvilla.

began to spread throughout the different native groups, and eventually the natives decided to fight back.

In October 1540, a chief named Tuscaloosa planned a surprise attack on de Soto's army. The battle at Mabila did not go well for Tuscaloosa's men. Most of them were killed alongside many soldiers in de Soto's army. Although de Soto won this battle, he decided to leave the area because his surviving soldiers were badly wounded.

It would take almost twenty years before another group of Spanish explorers entered the region again. Don Tristán de Luna y Arellano came with settlers who tried to establish a colony near Mobile Bay. Luna was also looking for gold. Like de Soto before him, Luna did not find it. Many of his people died from disease or hunger. So after three years, the Spanish colony was abandoned.

The French Colonists

In 1689, the explorer René-Robert Cavelier, often called Sieur de La Salle, traveled down the Mississippi River and claimed for France all the land around it. This included present-day Alabama. He named the land the Louisiana Territory. Ten years later, in 1699, two brothers, Pierre and Jean-Baptiste Le Moyne, landed on Dauphin Island in Mobile Bay, ready to take on their jobs as governors of the territory.

By 1702, the first permanent European settlement in Alabama was established at the mouth of Mobile Bay. Life there was not easy. There was very little food and many diseases. There were also constant battles with pirates and Spanish settlers who still lingered in the area.

These early French settlers tried hard to raise crops, but they found that they needed a lot more help with the labor. They brought over about six hundred slaves—the first black slaves to enter the region. Even this extra help did not save the settlers, though. The French might have starved to death had the Creeks not shared their food with them.

After a disastrous expedition, La Salle was killed by his own men in Texas in 1687.

Andrew Dexter was one of the founders of the city of Montgomery, which would eventually become Alabama's capital.

The French finally found they could make more money selling furs from wild animals, such as beavers. Unfortunately, British fur trappers were moving into the area, and the competition for the land and the fur trade grew very serious. The dispute over who had the right to hunt on the land erupted into what would be called the French and Indian War. Many Native Americans sided with the French as they fought the British. The French were defeated, though, and had to sign the Treaty of Paris of 1763. This forced the French to surrender all their land in the region, which included present-day Alabama. The British now controlled the region.

Statehood

After winning the French and Indian War, the British controlled the area of Alabama for fewer than twenty years. In the late 1770s, the British colonies on the Atlantic coast went to war for their independence from Great Britain. The colonists won the Revolutionary War and the new government signed another Treaty of Paris in 1783. The victory over Great Britain gave the newly formed

United States the right to the land east of the Mississippi River. Spain argued against this claim, stating that they still owned the southern coastline around Mobile. The United States did not have full control over the region. It was not until the end of the War of 1812 (fought between Great Britain and the United States) that the United States government finally gained control of all the land that today includes Alabama.

In 1817, the land was named the Territory of Alabama. Two years after that, Alabama become a state. Alabama was fully admitted to the United States on December 14, 1819. The new state's legislators, or lawmakers, first met in Huntsville. Cahaba was the next city to serve as Alabama's capital, until 1826 when Tuscaloosa was chosen. Montgomery was voted as the new state capital in 1846, and it is still Alabama's capital city today.

By the 1850s, Alabama's economy was booming, mostly because of cotton. People from all over the states came to Alabama, and many brought hundreds of slaves with them. This brought prosperity to Alabama, but it also brought problems.

As more settlers and farmers arrived, pressure was put on the native groups to give up their land. Unfair treaties between the United States and Native Americans were written. Native Americans were often forced to sign the treaties, and in many cases, the United States did not keep their promises. Most of the Native Americans who had once lived in Alabama were forced to move. Tens of thousands were sent west to Indian Territory, which was located in present-day Oklahoma. One of the most famous forced-removals of Native Americans was called the Trail of Tears.

Quick Facts

In 1830, US president Andrew Jackson signed the Indian Removal Act. The law let the US government negotiate with Indians and move them to federal territory in exchange for the Indians signing over their land.

Cotton plantations in the South were dependent on slave labor. Without the workers, the crops could not be harvested.

MAKING A SACHET

Alabama's residents often used chests to store such things as clothes and blankets. To keep things smelling fresh, they often used sachets, or cloth pouches filled with fragrant plants such as herbs or flowers. Follow these instructions to make your own sachet.

WHAT YOU NEED

2 pieces of cotton fabric. Each piece
    must be 3 inches by 4 inches
    (7.6 cm by 10 cm)
Pins
Scissors
Sewing needle
Thread
Narrow ribbon, about 5 to 6 inches
    (12.7–15 cm) long

Put one fabric piece on top of the other, with the outsides (or printed sides) facing each other. Pin the edges together on three sides.

Cut an 18-inch-(46 cm) long piece of thread and carefully thread it through the needle. Knot the end of the thread.

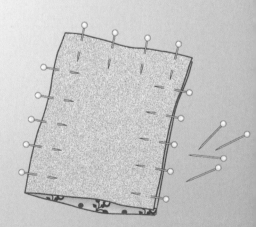

Using the needle and thread, stitch around the three pinned sides. You might need an adult to help you with the sewing. After your last stitch, make a knot in the thread and cut off the extra thread.

Carefully remove the pins and put them in a safe place where no one will get pricked.

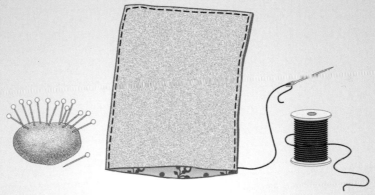

Gently turn the pouch right-side out.

To make the sachet smell nice, fill it half-full with potpourri. If you do not have potpourri, you can also stuff the sachet with scented dryer sheets or with cotton balls that have been lightly sprayed with a favorite perfume or cologne.

Tie the sachet closed using the ribbon. You can use your sachet to make your clothes smell nice or give it as a gift.

In 1838, thousands of Native Americans—mostly Cherokee—had to abandon their homes. They were forced to march west for more than 1,000 miles (1,609 km). During the march, almost 4,000 Native Americans died from cold, hunger, or disease.

Civil War and Reconstruction

By 1860, Alabama was producing a record amount of cotton. In order to handle all the labor, Alabama's farmers bought thousands of slaves. So many slaves lived in the state during this time that Alabama's black population almost equaled the white population. When Abraham Lincoln—who was in favor of abolishing, or ending, slavery—was elected president, many people in Alabama and other Southern states were upset. Part of the reason was because they did not want to lose their slaves. Slave labor was necessary for Southern plantations to be successful. Southern states made plans to secede, or break away, from the United States.

In 1861, leaders from the Southern states met in Montgomery and created a new nation called the Confederate States of America. Montgomery was the Confederacy's capital. Jefferson Davis, former US Senator from Mississippi, was elected president of the Confederacy. One year later, war broke out between Confederate soldiers and Union, or Northern, forces. Not all Alabamians favored the Confederacy. Some Alabamians did not believe in slavery. These people either hid in the northern hills of Alabama and refused to fight or they joined the Union army. Also, many slaves managed to run away, and some of them also joined the Northern forces.

There were no major battles fought on Alabamian soil. However, Union forces occupied several Alabama cities. Many Alabamians' lives were lost during the Civil War. There was a big battle in Mobile Bay

Quick Facts

The Jim Crow laws limited the legal rights of African Americans after the Civil War. The laws prevented many blacks from voting or holding public office. They also led to public schools, restaurants, bathrooms, and many other places being segregated, or separated by race.

because it was an important port through which the Confederate forces received supplies. The Union knew they had to take control of this port, so they fought the Confederate forces and won in 1864. A year later, the Civil War ended and the South admitted defeat.

Life was not easy after the Civil War for white or black people in the South. There was a shortage of food, farms and crops had been destroyed, and there were not many jobs available. Even though freed slaves enjoyed privileges they had never been given before, they did not enjoy them for very long. The Alabama government had signed the fourteenth amendment to the US Constitution, which guaranteed equal protection under the law to all citizens, including freed slaves. However, Alabama created its own state laws that took away many rights

The Battle of Mobile Bay was an important victory for the Union.

This illustration from 1861 shows crowds gathered in Montgomery to watch Jefferson Davis being inaugurated as president of the Confederacy.

from African Americans. Reconstruction, the name given to the rebuilding of the South, helped Alabama recover from the war. Life in Alabama was slowly improving, but not all of Alabama's citizens were benefiting from these changes.

Quick Facts

During the Great Depression, employment in Birmingham dropped from 100,000 jobs to only 15,000 full-time jobs. Some people believe the Great Depression affected Birmingham more than any other city in the United States.

Changing Times

Farming continued to be a major source of income for many Alabamians at the end of the 1800s. The processing of iron in northeastern Alabama created new jobs and a new city. Birmingham, located in the heart of the mining lands, was founded in 1871.

Another important industry at this time was cotton textiles. Cotton textiles were used to make things like sheets, clothing, and towels. Railroads, which had been built during Reconstruction, helped Alabama's industries by providing transportation for goods. The products were taken from the factories to other cities or to Mobile Bay, where they were shipped out of the state.

During the first half of the twentieth century, an insect called the boll weevil destroyed much of Alabama's cotton crops. New food crops, such as peanuts, were planted. This helped to save many people from having to close down their farms. Alabama's economy was also helped when the United States entered World War I. American factories and farms produced supplies that the troops needed during the war.

Much of Alabama's cotton was sent to the state's textile mills. At the mills, the fiber was used to make clothing, blankets, and other material.

In 1929, however, the American economy took a downward turn. The Great Depression hit the country and many stores and banks went out of business. Most Americans lost their jobs. Farms failed and had to be closed down. Many Alabamians left the state to look for jobs. The US government did what it could to help the people, establishing work programs throughout the country. These programs created jobs that had the workers building and repairing roads and bridges, or working in lumber mills in the nation's forests.

The United States entered World War II in 1941, and this also helped the country's economy. Factories and farms again had to provide needed supplies for American troops. States' economies, including Alabama's, improved.

In the 1950s, a new industry brought prosperity to parts of Alabama. Huntsville became an important center for rocket and space research.

Men and boys of all ages worked in Alabama's mines. In the early 1900s, Alabama's mined materials were mostly used for suppplies for the war efforts.

Alabama's cities, such as Montgomery, continued to grow in the 1950s and 1960s.

This industry created more jobs for Alabamians. For example, the Saturn V rocket was developed at NASA's (National Aeronautics and Space Administration's) Space Flight Center in Huntsville. In 1969, a Saturn V rocket propelled Apollo 11 into space, where Neil Armstrong became the first man to walk on the moon.

Around the same time the space program was developing, African Americans began fighting for their civil rights. They had grown tired of being denied the same rights as white citizens. They fought against segregation, which was a system that separated whites from blacks. Because of segregation, African Americans could not shop at some stores, could not eat at certain restaurants, and had to sit in the backs of public buses. Many African Americans could only hold low-paying jobs because they were not given better opportunities. Black children could not attend the same schools as white children, and the all-black schools were not given enough government money and did not have the same programs or supplies as white schools. In many cases, African Americans in parts of the United States were still not able to vote in elections.

As a result of Rosa Parks' brave actions, the Supereme Court decided that segregation on Montgomery's city buses was illegal.

In this photograph, Martin Luther King Jr. and his wife, Coretta Scott King, are marching with other civil rights activists through a neighborhood in Selma in 1965.

The civil rights movement, in which many African Americans and whites led peaceful marches and protests, was very active in Alabama. In 1955, Rosa Parks refused to go to the back of a Montgomery city bus to give up her seat to a white man. She was arrested for this, which led to the Montgomery bus boycott. During the boycott, Alabama citizens—black and white—who opposed segregation refused to use Montgomery's buses. In 1956, the United States Supreme Court—the highest court in the country—declared segregated bus seating illegal. This marked the beginning of the civil rights movement.

Martin Luther King Jr., a pastor of a church in Montgomery, brought the hardships of everyday life of blacks to the attention of people throughout the United States and the world. In 1965, Dr. King led one of the most significant marches in the fight for civil rights. This march began in Selma and ended in Montgomery, 80 miles (129 km) away. The people in this march were fighting for African Americans' right to vote. It would be a long, hard battle, but eventually African Americans would gain their equal rights.

Modern Alabama

From the end of the twentieth century and into the first decades of the twenty-first century, Alabama has undergone some changes. The population increased and new residents began living in different parts of the state. In the early 1900s, most Alabamians lived in rural communities and held jobs related to farming and agriculture. During the last half of the century, though, more than 60 percent of the population moved to the cities or the areas right outside the cities. This was a major shift for Alabama, which had previously been a very rural state. From 1970 on, people were moving off their farms in increasing numbers. They settled in the cities to find nonagricultural jobs, such as those in manufacturing and social services.

This caused an increase in suburban areas around Alabama's larger cities. Many counties around Alabama's cities doubled in population. Counties with a more rural setting lost half or more of the people who used to live there. Instead of being spread out throughout the state, people were living in clusters in urban areas. While this was good for the cities' economies, this also meant that problems such as air pollution, traffic jams, and the need for larger schools became worse. Meanwhile, the rural areas were facing a rise in poverty as more people left the region and stores and businesses were forced to close.

Today, people are searching for solutions to help the rural counties find ways to make money and to keep Alabama's city dwellers' environment clean and safe. Officials are trying to attract new industries to provide more jobs, both in urban and rural areas. Other people are focusing on how to adjust to the swiftly growing cities.

Although the twenty-first century is bringing a lot of change to Alabama, people who live there still enjoy some of the same things that have always made Alabama a great state. There are still large areas of well-preserved forests and many miles (km) of rivers. Alabama farmers can still make a living on the fertile

When Hurricane Katrina struck land in 2005, many Gulf Coastal states, including Alabama, were hit hard. The hurricane caused millions of dollars in damage, and many homes and lives were lost.

Young people have an opportunity to learn about spacecraft at the United States Space Camp in Huntsvillle.

soil by growing cotton and peanuts and raising livestock. Birmingham remains a major city, not only in producing steel, but also in providing services for all the people of the state. In Huntsville, which has been nicknamed Rocket City, USA, scientists continue to research better equipment for America's space program. Alabama is growing in many different ways, and its people are hard at work to make sure those changes are for the better.

Important Dates

★ **10,000 to 7,000 BCE**
Paleo-Indians live in Alabama's caves.

★ **700 to 1300 CE** Modern
Native culture develops, including
groups such as the Creek.

★ **1519** Alonso Álvarez de Pineda
becomes first European to enter Mobile Bay.

★ **1540** Hernando de Soto explores
Alabama in search of gold.

★ **1559** Tristán de Luna y Arellano builds
a temporary settlement in Mobile Bay.

★ **1689** Explorer Sieur de La Salle
travels down the Mississippi River and
claims all the land around the Mississippi
River, including present-day Alabama,
for France.

★ **1702** The first permanent non-Native
settlement is established at Mobile Bay.

★ **1763** The French are defeated and
sign the Treaty of Paris.

★ **1763** They lose their rights to land
that includes present-day Alabama.

★ **1817** Alabama becomes an official
territory of the United States.

★ **1819** Alabama becomes a state on
December 14.

★ **1850s** Cotton becomes an important
crop for the state.

★ **1861** Alabama votes to secede from
the Union and joins the Confederacy.

★ **1865** The Civil War ends and
Alabama rejoins the Union.

★ **1955** Rosa Parks refuses to sit at the
back of a city bus and the Montgomery bus
boycott begins.

★ **1965** Reverend Martin Luther
King Jr. leads a protest march from
Selma to Montgomery.

★ **2001** Condoleezza Rice, born in
Birmingham, becomes the first woman
to ever hold the office of National
Security Advisor.

★ **2005** Hurricane Katrina causes
widespread damage along the Alabama
coast.

★ **2010** The *Deepwater Horizon* oil
rig sinks in the Gulf of Mexico. Over 87
days, nearly 5 million barrels of oil spill in
the Gulf, affecting Alabama's marine life,
businesses, and tourism industry

★ **2011** An EF4 tornado destroys
parts of Birmingham and Tuscaloosa,
killing 64 people.

The People

Since the Civil War, the population of Alabama has grown from more than one million to almost five million people. Throughout this time, the state has seen many changes. People from other parts of the country and from around the world have made Alabama their home. Residents have moved from rural areas to urban areas, causing Alabama's cities and suburbs to grow and expand. Today, most Alabamians live in the state's largest cities, which include Birmingham, Mobile, Huntsville, Montgomery, Tuscaloosa, Florence, Anniston, and Gadsden.

The largest portion of Alabama's population is Caucasian or white. Around 70 percent of the state's residents are of European descent. (This includes people of French, British, and German ancestry, to name just a few.) Some residents are immigrants from those countries, while others may have parents, grandparents, or ancestors from Europe. Several Alabamian families can trace their roots all the way back to European settlers who first came to the region more than one hundred years ago.

Influences from these different European cultures can be found not only in Alabama's people but also in the architecture (the buildings), in cultural events, and in the names of towns and counties throughout the state. For example,

Colorful flowers bloom outside a Civil War-era mansion in Eufaula.

Some Alabamians are descended from the first European settlers who made their homes in the region.

Alabama's French culture is reflected in Mobile's celebration of Mardi Gras. The Creole culture, which is a mixture of French, African, and Native American cultures, is also present in Alabama. There are Alabamians of Creole descent, and several restaurants in the state serve traditional Creole food.

Place names in Alabama also reflect the state's European ancestry. For example, Cullman County was named after John G. Cullman, a German immigrant who settled in northern Alabama and encouraged other Germans to follow him.

Native Americans

From 10,000 BC to 7000 BC the Paleo-Indians were the first people to live in Alabama. Many of these people did not build permanent homes, but instead traveled with the seasons in search of food. By 1000 BC, the descendants of these early peoples had lifestyles that were different. These natives started to build permanent settlements. They planted crops and for hunting, used bows and arrows—tools that the earliest of the Paleo-Indians did not have.

Thousands of years later, native life changed even more. Native groups started working and living close together to improve their hunting success. Organized communities and settlements were developed. In the 1500s, the natives were introduced to European influences. As Europeans came to search for gold or explore the land, many natives were killed by the diseases the Europeans carried or in battles against the newcomers.

When the Europeans returned to the Alabama area in 1700 to try to create permanent settlements, the largest native group they found there was the Muskogee, who were also known as the Creeks. By 1814, the Creeks had signed away most of their land to the US government through many treaties. Most of the Native Americans were then forcibly removed from Alabama. A few Alabamian natives escaped this removal plan. One of these groups is the Poarch Band of Creek Indians.

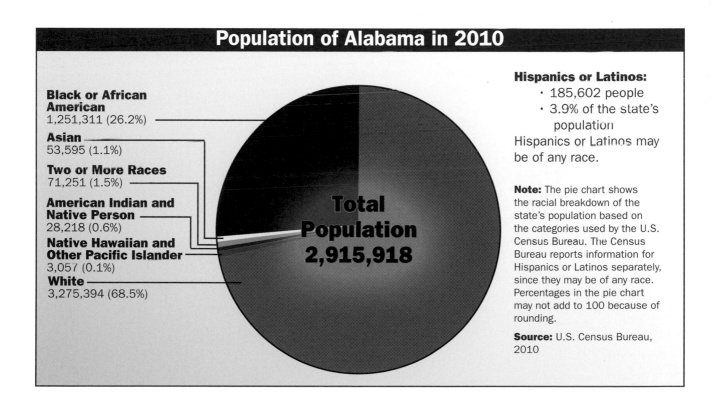

Population of Alabama in 2010

Black or African American
1,251,311 (26.2%)

Asian
53,595 (1.1%)

Two or More Races
71,251 (1.5%)

American Indian and Native Person
28,218 (0.6%)

Native Hawaiian and Other Pacific Islander
3,057 (0.1%)

White
3,275,394 (68.5%)

Total Population 2,915,918

Hispanics or Latinos:
- 185,602 people
- 3.9% of the state's population

Hispanics or Latinos may be of any race.

Note: The pie chart shows the racial breakdown of the state's population based on the categories used by the U.S. Census Bureau. The Census Bureau reports information for Hispanics or Latinos separately, since they may be of any race. Percentages in the pie chart may not add to 100 because of rounding.

Source: U.S. Census Bureau, 2010

Today there are about 3,095 members of the Poarch Band of Creeks who still live on their land about 60 miles (97 km) northeast of Mobile. The Poarch Creeks are not the only native people still living in Alabama, though. About 7 percent of the state's total population is of Native American heritage. That means over 33,000 Native American Alabamians make their homes throughout the state. Some live and work in rural communities, while others run businesses or have jobs in the cities.

The growth of Alabama's cities, like Birmingham, encouraged more people from different parts of the country and the world to move to the Heart of Dixie.

Fiesta, the state's largest celebration of Hispanic heritage and culture, is held each year in Birmingham.

Latinos

Although explorers from Spain were the first Europeans to land on the soil of Alabama, people who are from Spain or have Spanish ancestors make up a very small portion of the population. However, a growing minority are the Latinos. These are residents whose families are from Mexico, Cuba, Puerto Rico, and other countries in Central and South America. Sometimes these residents are also called Hispanic Americans, and they make up about 4 percent of the population.

In the past ten years, however, the population of Latino Alabamians has grown more than any other minority group. Many Latinos have come to the state to attend the schools, or work and own successful businesses. Several Latino families have been living in Alabama for decades. Some experts are predicting that in the future, there will be more Hispanics and Latinos than African Americans living in Alabama.

Famous Alabamians

Helen Keller: Speaker and Author

Helen Keller was born in 1880 in Tuscumbia. At an early age, Helen lost her sight and hearing. Despite her inability to see or hear, Helen graduated with honors from Radcliffe College. Keller spent much of her life trying to help others—especially people with disabilities or people who did not have equal rights. She became a famous writer and speaker and traveled around the world.

Tim Cook: Businessperson

Tim Cook was born in Robertson, near Mobile, in 1960. He earned a degree in industrial engineering from Auburn University in 1982. Today, he is the CEO of Apple Inc., the company that produces iPods, iPads, and Mac computers, among other things. Apple Inc. is one of the largest companies in the world and made $156 billion in 2012. Cook took over as Apple's CEO when Steve Jobs passed away in 2011. Today, Cook is working to create new products and lead Apple Inc. into the future.

Rosa Parks: Civil Rights Activist

A native of Tuskegee, Rosa Parks is often called the mother of the civil rights movement. She was very active in fighting for equal rights for African Americans and is best remembered for refusing to give up her seat on a bus. Her action led to a citywide boycott of Montgomery's buses. The boycott, in turn, triggered widespread protests against segregation all across the United States. Rosa Parks died in 2005.

Condoleezza Rice: Politician and Diplomat

Condoleezza Rice was born in Birmingham in 1954. As a child, she experienced segregation and discrimination. She also watched the civil rights movement develop. In college, she became interested in politics. In 2001 she became the first woman to hold the position of national security advisor. In 2005 she became the US secretary of state, under President George W. Bush. Rice was the first African-American woman to hold the position.

Jesse Owens: Olympic Athlete

In 1913, Jesse Owens was born in Danville. A strong athlete throughout his younger years, when he was only twenty-two years old, Owens set three world records in the 220-yard low hurdles race and in the broad jump. He qualified for the 1936 Olympics, in which he also set records in the 100-meter race and in the broad jump. Jesse Owens became the fourth American to win three or more gold medals in the Olympic Games. Owens' triumphs were especially notable because he lived during a time when African Americans had very few rights and privileges. In 1976, Owens was awarded the Medal of Freedom—one of the nations' highest honors. He died in 1980.

Harper Lee: Author

Nelle Harper Lee was born in 1926 in Monroeville. She is best known for her Pulitzer Prize-wining novel, *To Kill a Mockingbird*, which has been called one of the most important books of the twentieth century. Her novel tells the story of an African-American man who is wrongly accused of a crime, the white lawyer who defends him, and the relationship between the lawyer and his children. The story is set in Alabama and more than ten million copies of the novel have been sold all over the world.

Asian Americans

About 1.2 percent of Alabama's population is Asian or Asian American. Some of the countries from which these Alabama citizens or their ancestors have come include Vietnam, Japan, China, Laos, the Philippines, and Cambodia. There are some Asian Americans who have lived in Alabama for many generations, while others have arrived only recently. Much of Alabama's Asian-American population is concentrated in counties such as Madison, Mobile, Lee, Dale, and Tuscaloosa.

Each year the Alabama Asian Cultures Foundation holds a festival in Birmingham celebrating Asian cultures and food.

The Birmingham Civil Rights Institute features an exhibit on the 16th Street Baptist Church bombing, which killed four young girls in 1963.

African Americans

In 1721, aboard the ship the *Africane*, more than one hundred black slaves were delivered to their Alabama owners. Later, as the cotton crop gained importance to the Alabama economy, more slaves entered the state. By the middle of the nineteenth century, there were almost a half a million slaves living in the state. Not all blacks in Alabama were slaves, though. There was also a small population of freed slaves.

After the end of the Civil War, all slaves were freed, but many of them continued to live close to their former owners, who gave them land on which to plant crops. There was a catch to this plan, though. These freed slaves, who were called sharecroppers, had to give the landowners a large portion of the food they raised as a form of rent payment for this land. In many instances, they were allowed to keep only enough food to eat, and had none left over to sell for extra money.

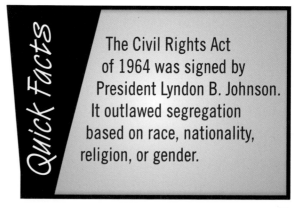

Quick Facts

The Civil Rights Act of 1964 was signed by President Lyndon B. Johnson. It outlawed segregation based on race, nationality, religion, or gender.

Young Alabamians sing traditional songs that honor the state's past. Music has a long history in Alabama.

One of the main problems for blacks living in the South was segregation, which prevented them from doing many things that white people were allowed to do. Through the efforts of people like Dr. Martin Luther King Jr. and members of such groups as the National Association for the Advancement of Colored People (NAACP), African Americans finally won their civil rights as segregation was made illegal.

Many African Americans still make their homes in Alabama and represent the largest minority in the state, with about 26.5 percent of the population. Like all state residents, African-American Alabamians play an important part in the state's history, economy, and culture. African Americans from Alabama have made many contributions to the country in a variety of professional fields. Condoleezza Rice was the first woman to serve as the country's national security advisor. Mae Jemison was the first African-American woman astronaut. In professional basketball, Leeds native Charles Barkley was an impressive athlete. In the entertainment industry, Nell Carter from Birmingham was an award-winning actress and singer who became famous on television and on Broadway.

No matter where Alabamians come from, one thing many people in the state seem to have in common is a love of music. Alabama is home to hundreds of musicians and musical festivals. Musicians in Alabama are said to be greatly

The Heart of Dixie is filled with people from different backgrounds, working together to make Alabama a great state.

responsible for developing both blues and country music. You can also find zydeco, or Cajun, music from the French Creole people, German polkas, Appalachian fiddling, Hispanic mariachi, American rock and roll, and African-American-inspired jazz and soul. Alabama is also famous for producing music stars such as Nat King Cole, Hank Williams, Lionel Ritchie, Emmylou Harris, and the Temptations.

Alabama is and has been home to famous people, such as entertainers, politicians, and civil rights leaders, and everyday Alabamians like school teachers, bank tellers, and store owners. Alabama residents may be descended from people who settled the land hundreds of years ago, or they may have moved to the state more recently. They may come from different cultures, but Alabamians from a variety of ethnic backgrounds love their state. Some may live in their same hometown all their lives, while others might travel far away. No matter where Alabamians live, no matter how far away some might roam, Alabama will always be where their hearts are.

In Their Own Words

By growing up in Alabama, I had a melting pot of the whole pie: R&B, gospel, country.

—Recording artist Lionel Richie

Calendar of Events

★ **Alabama Chicken and Egg Festival**

Over three days in April, the town of Moulton celebrates the state's agricultural roots with the Chicken and Egg Festival. There are music performances, arts and crafts, and, of course, food vendors selling many different kinds of chicken dishes!

★ **Rattlesnake Rodeo**

Every spring, the town of Opp holds a Rattlesnake Rodeo. There are concerts, beauty pageants, dance contests, and other fun activities. Prizes are given to hunters who catch the most eastern diamondback rattlesnakes. However, some people in the state are worried that too many snakes are being killed. They are trying to get the leaders of Opp to make the festival more wildlife-friendly.

★ **The Helen Keller Festival**

In June, Tuscumbia honors Helen Keller with a fun festival that lasts five days. There are many activities to enjoy, such as a parade through the town, arts and crafts booths, puppet shows, and sports tournaments. You can also watch a live performance of *The Miracle Worker*, the famous play about Keller's life.

★ **Mardi Gras in Mobile**

Each year, Mobile celebrates Mardi Gras with parades, balls, and parties. The celebration stretches over a two-week period, though some groups begin holding their parties as early as November!

★ Alabama Deep Sea Fishing Rodeo

In July, thousands of anglers from across the country fish off the coast of Alabama in the Gulf of Mexico. The 2011 event was, for a time, the largest fishing tournament in the world, according to Guinness World Records.

★ Renaissance Faire

In October, Florence puts on a Renaissance Faire to celebrate Europe's culture and history during the Middle Ages, and most fair participants are dressed in traditional clothing. At the fair, you can eat great food, listen to live music performances, and watch knights fight in mock battles.

★ National Peanut Festival

Dothan is known for its favorite crop, the peanut. In November the city holds a National Peanut Festival. The celebration lasts for two weeks and has a carnival, fair, parade, and beauty pageant. Dothan is often called the Peanut Capital of America.

★ Christmas on the River

Every year in the beginning of December, tens of thousands of people come to Demopolis for the city's Christmas on the River celebration. The main attraction is the parade of lighted floats that drift down the river at night. The festival also includes candlelight tours of historic homes, a children's parade, an arts and crafts show, a barbeque cook-off, and fireworks displays.

How the Government Works

There are different levels of government in the Heart of Dixie. At the national level, Alabama elects two people to serve in the US Senate and seven people to serve in the House of Representatives. The number of seats each state holds in the House of Representatives is based on its population. Alabama has had seven seats since 1970.

Nearly all of Alabama's towns and cities have their own local government. They are not all alike, though. Some cities or towns have mayors and city councils who are elected by the residents. Other cities have a commission or a city manager. Whatever form it takes, local government is responsible for issues that are specific to the town or city. These issues may include land use, school budgets, housing plans and problems, and local law enforcement.

Based on where they are located, Alabama's towns and cities are grouped together into counties. The state has 67 counties. County government is responsible for handling issues that affect multiple towns and cities. Elected county officials include tax assessors, boards of education, county commissioners, and certain judges.

The State Capitol is in Montgomery.

Alabama's Constitutions

Each state in the Union has its own constitution, which is a legal document that contains a series of laws by which the state is governed. Over the years, the people in Alabama's legislature have written six different constitutions.

The first constitution was written when Alabama became a state in 1819. A new constitution replaced it in 1861, around the time of the Civil War. A third was created after the Civil War in 1865, only to be replaced by the fourth constitution in 1868, which was written during Reconstruction. The fifth constitution was written in 1875. And finally, in 1901, the constitution that is still in use today was put into practice.

Alabama's current constitution, with all its amendments, or additions, is the longest constitution in the world. It is 375,000 words long, while most other state constitutions are only about 26,000 words long. Some people in Alabama think the state constitution is too long and too detailed. There are many people who are debating whether Alabama should have a new constitution. These people believe a new constitution would do things such as removing laws that allowed discrimination based on race, and changing laws so that more power would be granted to Alabama's cities.

How a Bill Becomes a Law

According to the Alabama state constitution, no law can be passed unless it first becomes a bill. A bill is a proposed law that has been written out in the proper legal form. There are steps that a bill must go through in order to become a law.

EXECUTIVE ★ ★ ★ ★ ★ ★ ★ ★ ★

The governor, who is the head of the executive branch, is responsible for making sure laws are enforced. He or she can sign a law into practice or veto (reject) a law that the legislature has passed. Alabama's governor is elected into office and may serve two terms in a row. He or she is eligible to serve again after four years out of office. The executive branch also includes the state's lieutenant governor, secretary of state, attorney general, treasurer, auditor, and commissioner of agriculture industries.

LEGISLATIVE ★ ★ ★ ★ ★ ★ ★ ★

The state legislature is called the General Assembly. It is made up of two separate houses called the state senate and the state house of representatives. There are 35 senators and 105 state representatives. Each of these officials is elected into office by Alabama citizens. The legislature is responsible for creating new laws.

JUDICIAL ★ ★ ★ ★ ★ ★ ★ ★ ★

The judicial branch is headed by the State Supreme Court, which is the highest court in the state. This court is led by a chief justice and eight associate judges. Other lower courts include the court of civil appeals and the court of criminal appeals. The responsibility of the judicial branch is to hear trials.

Different rooms in the State Capitol hold pieces of Alabama history—from portraits to furniture used by the state's first legislators.

First, the bill is presented to one of the houses of the General Assembly. It is then assigned an official number. The bill is then read to the members of that house on three different occasions. The first time it is read, only the title of the bill is mentioned. Then the bill is discussed by a special committee of senators or representatives. For example, if the bill involves a state health issue, then it will be sent to the special committee that focuses on health. If the bill involves education, it will be sent to the special committee for educational issues. It is the committee's job to decide if the bill should be read for the second time in front of all the senators or representatives. Sometimes bills get no further than a committee reading. If the committee approves the bill, though, the second reading is done by mentioning only the title of the bill. It is not until the third reading that the entire bill may be read to all members.

After the third reading, members of the house or senate may debate the bill and the issues it addresses. Changes can be made to the bill. When they are satisfied with the bill, the senators or representatives vote on it. Voting is done differently in the senate than in the house. Since there are only 35 members in the senate, most times the senators' names are called out in alphabetical order, and they give their vote out loud. The process in the house is different because there are 105 representatives, and it might take too long. So representatives vote electronically by pushing buttons located on their desks. If enough senators or representatives vote in favor of the bill, it moves to the other house. For example, if the bill was first introduced and approved in the senate, it then goes to the house of representatives.

The bill undergoes mostly the same process in the other half of the General Assembly. The bill is discussed, debated, and possibly changed. If enough officials support the bill, it is passed on to the governor for approval. If the governor approves the bill, he or she signs it into law. The governor can also veto, or reject, the bill. The bill can still become law if enough senators and representatives vote to override the governor.

Contacting Lawmakers

★ ★ ★ ★ ★ ★ ★ ★ ★ ★ ★ ★

If you are interested in contacting Alabama's state legislators, go to

http://www.legislature.state.al.us/

You can search for legislators and their contact information by name, zip code, or district.

Making a Difference

Alabama's state legislature is there to serve Alabamians. In fact, many ideas for bills or laws come from state residents. They consider issues that affect their communities and then point these issues out to their state legislators. For example, the idea to make the blackberry the official state fruit came from young students in Baldwin County. Both the senate and the house of representatives passed the bill, and in 2004 the blackberry became Alabama's state fruit.

Making a Living

Agriculture

Alabama has long been an agricultural state. This means that at one time, most of the state's money came from products raised on farms and plantations. Until the twentieth century, most of Alabama's money came from cotton. Since the boll weevil destroyed many cotton crops, though, other types of crops have been planted. For instance, Alabama is the third-largest producer of peanuts and peanut products in the United States, behind Georgia and Texas. About 300,000 acres (121,406 ha) of soybeans were harvested in 2011. Other crops that are raised in large amounts include corn, sweet potatoes, watermelons, beans, and peas. Farmers also produce a lot of peaches, pecans, blueberries, and tomatoes.

Not all Alabama crops are used as food or in manufacturing. The state also provides plants that go toward the nursery industry. Garden shops throughout the state and around the country sell plants and flowers that have been grown in Alabama. These include azalea bushes, many types of flowers, small trees, and ground cover like ivy.

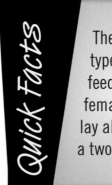

Quick Facts

The boll weevil is a type of beetle that feeds on cotton. The female boll weevil can lay about 200 eggs over a two-week period.

A natural gas plant towers over a cotton field. Both cotton and natural gas are very important to Alabama's economy.

RECIPE FOR ALABAMA PECAN LOGS

Pecans are a popular product in the South. Follow this recipe to make a tasty pecan treat.

Ingredients:
1/2 pound (227 g) sweet butter
1/2 cup powdered sugar
2 cups chopped pecans
1/2 teaspoon salt
1 cup flour
1 teaspoon vanilla

Have an adult preheat the oven to 325°F (163°C). Grease a large cookie sheet with vegetable oil or shortening.

Ask an adult to help you mix the butter until it is smooth. Slowly add the sugar, salt, flour, and vanilla.

When those ingredients are well-mixed, stir in the pecans.

Take a heaping spoonful of the batter and put it on a plate. Roll it into the shape of a log and place it on the cookie sheet. When the sheet is full, place it in the oven.

Bake the logs for 15 to 20 minutes. During this time, keep checking on them to make sure they do not burn.

When they are done, let them cool. Enjoy your nutty treat!

The boll weevil, seen here, is native to Central America. It arrived in Alabama in 1909.

Crops are not the only way farmers make money. More money in agriculture is made in livestock. In 2013, Alabama farmers owned more than 1.2 million cows. Some of these cows are used on dairy farms, but most are used for food. When the cattle are old enough and big enough, they are shipped to centers in Alabama or neighboring states. Alabama's biggest farm product, according to the U.S. Department of Agriculture, is broiler chickens. These small chickens are grown and sold as food and make up about 55 percent of the state's farm income.

A new type of farming in Alabama involves fish. Alabama has about 22,000 acres (8,903 ha) of fish farms. Farmers watch over the fish, making sure they eat a good diet and do not get sick. When the fish are big enough, they are sold to places like restaurants and grocery stores. In Alabama, a lot of catfish are raised in fish farms. Today, Alabama ranks second in the United States in annual catfish

Catfish farms are a growing part of the state's agricultural industry.

sales, and the industry is growing quickly. Some fish farmers also raise ornamental fish. These fish include koi—a large type of carp—and goldfish. People sometimes build ponds in their yards and stock them with koi. Smaller goldfish are usually kept in aquariums in people's homes.

Most of Alabama's fish, however, are still caught in open waters such as the Gulf of Mexico or in Alabama's rivers and reservoirs. There are river-caught catfish, which is one of the most popular fish in Alabama, but there are also saltwater fish such as groupers and snappers that are caught in the Gulf.

Alabama's shrimp and shellfish industry used to provide millions of dollars to the state's economy. Unfortunately, this industry was hit hard by both Hurricane Katrina and the 2010 Gulf oil spill. However, Alabamians are working hard to make this industry profitable once again.

Mining

Alabama has large deposits of coal and limestone. These are used to make iron and steel, two important products for Alabama's economy. Alabama is the only state that has all the ingredients located within the state to make iron and steel. Alabama is the largest supplier of cast-iron and steel pipe products.

The business of drilling for resources such as oil and natural gas has been expanding in the state over the past twenty years. Today, Alabama ranks 14th in the country as a major producer of natural gas. Natural gas is used to create energy and heat for homes and businesses.

A worker checks on an oil pump.

This tugboat is pushing a barge of wood chips along the Tombigbee River.

Manufacturing

More than 246,000 Alabamians work in the state's manufacturing industry. Items that are made in Alabama include everything from food and tobacco products to leather, paper, and wood products. Chemicals, automobiles, plastics, computers, jewelry, toys, and furniture are also manufactured in Alabama.

Many companies from other parts of the world, such as Japan and Korea, have built car factories in Alabama in recent years. Other large companies in the state manufacture important government-related products such as aerospace equipment and missiles.

There are also large companies in Alabama that process food. This includes human food such as candy and ice cream, but also pet food. Other companies use Alabama's cotton crops to make textiles, or materials for things such as curtains, towels, and clothes.

Alabama's lumber industry is profitable. A large amount of wood is shipped to other parts of the country. Alabama also has factories to process the wood, turning it into useful products like wood chips, furniture, or paper.

The Service Industry

The service industry includes people who provide a service to others. For example, people who work at grocery stores, insurance companies, schools, hospitals, gas stations, hotels, amusement parks, movie theaters, shopping malls, and police and fire departments are all a part of the service industry.

Tourism is a huge part of Alabama's service industry. Alabama's natural beauty attracts tourists from other states and people from all over the world. Its historic sites and busy cities also bring in visitors. Visitors who come to Alabama stay in hotels, eat in restaurants, buy gas, and spend money on entertainment and souvenirs. All of this money helps the state's economy and jobs are created and maintained to support the tourism industry. Today, the tourism industry contributes more than $9.3 billion to Alabama's economy.

Visitors to Alabama can learn about the state's history at sites like Constitution Hall Village, in Huntsville.

Products & Resources

Catfish

Catfish farming has become one of Alabama's fastest-growing agricultural activities in recent years. There are many different kinds of catfish, but the channel catfish is the most common type raised on the fish farms. Although they can grow to almost 50 pounds (23 kg), most channel catfish weigh between 10 and 20 pounds (4.5–9 kg).

Steel

Alabama's first steel mill opened in 1880, and ten years later, steel was Alabama's biggest industry. Today, steel continues to be an important product in Alabama. Many products are made of steel, but some of the most decorative steel products from Alabama are wrought iron furniture pieces. The wrought iron is twisted and curled to make interesting designs.

Eggs

The average American eats more than two hundred eggs each year. That is about as many eggs as one healthy chicken can produce in a year. Alabama has a lot of chickens and a lot of eggs. On large farms, chickens are housed in big buildings. The eggs from these chickens are collected by machines. The eggs are sorted by size and packaged into cartons. Alabama eggs are then shipped out to grocery stores throughout the state and around the country.

Wood Products

About 70 percent of Alabama is still covered in forests, giving the state the second-most extensive forest cover in the United States. Some of the trees that are grown in Alabama's forests are made into paper products. The trees are sent to a mill, where they are trimmed, chopped, and boiled into a pulp. Then the pulp is laid out on large screens and dried. Later the dried pulp is pressed to form paper.

Fishing

Sport fishing is part of the state's tourism industry. Alabamians, as well as people from other places, enjoy fishing in Alabama's rivers, lakes, and streams. Many also take big boats out into the Gulf and spend the day catching big tuna or swordfish.

Aerospace and Flight Research

Researchers at the Marshall Space Flight Center in Huntsville produced the rocket that propelled the first landing on the moon. That is not all they have done over the years. They have also produced the tools that maintained the Hubble Space Telescope, and their designs were used to create the International Space Station. The Marshall Space Flight Center provides many jobs for Alabamians.

Alabama's Industries & Workers (April 2013)

Industry	Number of People Working in That Industry	Percentage of Labor Force Working in That Industry
Mining and Logging	12,500	0.6%
Construction	79,500	3.7%
Manufacturing	246,900	11.3%
Trade, Transportation, and Utilities	366,300	16.8%
Information	21,200	1%
Financial Activities	92,300	4.2%
Professional and Business Services	219,900	10%
Education and Health Services	221,900	10.2%
Leisure and Hospitality	178,500	8.2%
Other Services	79,800	3.7%
Government	373,700	17.2%
Farming	285,200	13.1%
Totals	**2,177,700**	**100%**

Facing the Future

In 2010, as oil gushed into the Gulf of Mexico, many people were worried the oil spill would damage Alabama's beaches beyond repair and destroy the state's fishing and tourism industries. While the oil spill did, indeed, cause a great deal of damage, the people of Alabama remained resilient. In the years since the oil spill, they have worked hard to restore their beaches and environment and encourage tourists to visit their beautiful state.

The people of Alabama have faced troubled times before, from the Civil War and the unrest of the civil rights movement to natural disasters such as Hurricane Katrina and the tornado that ripped through Tuscaloosa. Much like the Great Depression of the 1930s, the recession of the early 2000s is hitting Alabama hard. However, Alabamians continue to persevere. They remain hopeful and do their best to help their fellow citizens. What else would you expect from the Heart of Dixie?

State Flag & Seal

In 1895 Alabama selected an official state flag. The flag displays a red diagonal cross on a white background. The flag was designed after the Confederate battle flag used during the Civil War.

Alabama's state seal shows a rough map of Alabama, its rivers, and the territories around Alabama. (These territories would later become states.) This seal was originally used as the territorial seal in the 1800s. It was made the official state seal in 1819, but was replaced by a different seal in the late 1860s. In 1939 Alabama's state government decided to use the original seal, and it has been the official seal ever since.

ALABAMA

Pickwick Lake
Florence
72
U.S. Space and Rocket Center and Space Camp
Russell Cave National Monument
65
Tennessee River
Huntsville
Wheeler Lake
Sequoyah Caverns
Birthplace of Helen Keller
43
157
Decatur
Cathedral Caverns State Park
75
Little River Canyon National Preserve
24
William B. Bankhead National Forest
31
Wheeler National Wildlife Refuge
431
Dismals Canyon
78
276
59
Weiss Lake
Natural Bridge
Lewis Smith Lake
5
Gadsden
278
17
Rickwood Caverns State Park
H. Neely Henry Lake
Anniston
20
Talladega Superspeedway
Sipsey River
Birmingham
Bankhead Lake
Logan Martin Lake
Cheaha Mountain
82
Tuscaloosa
459
De Soto Caverns Park
77
R.L. Harris Reservoir
431
West Point Lake
20 59
Black Warrior River
Coosa River
9
Lay Lake
Talladega National Forest
85
Mitchell Lake
21
Lake Martin
Horseshoe Bend National Military Park
Auburn
85
First White House of the Confederacy
Fort Toulouse/ Jackson State Historic Park
280
Demopolis
Old Cahawba Site of First State Capital
Selma
Montgomery
Tuskegee
Tombigbee River
80
William "Bill" Dannelly Reservoir
82
28
Eufaula
Alabama River
10
331
231
Walter F. George Reservoir
84
31
51
Choctawhatchee River
10
Jackson
65
55
Gantt Lake
95
Poarch Creek Indian Reservation
Point "A" Lake
Lake Tholocco
Dothan
Opp
Enterprise
45
59
41
29
Conecuh National Forest
217
Atmore
Big Creek Lake
Mobile River
112
Mobile
10
Foley
Mobile Bay
Bon Secour Bay
Perdido Bay
Mississippi Sound
INTRACOASTAL WATERWAY
GULF OF MEXICO

miles
0   40

Interstate Highway	City or Town		Highest Point in the State
U.S. Highway	Indian Reservation		National Preserve
State Highway	National Monument		Historic Site
State Capital	Wildlife Refuge		National Forest

State Song

Alabama

words by Julia Strudwick Tutwiler and music by Edna Gockel Gussen

1. Al - a-bam - a, Al - a-bam - a, We will aye be true to thee,

From thy South-ern shores where grow-eth By the _ sea thy or - ange tree.

To _ thy North-ern vale where flow-eth Deep and blue_ thy Ten-nes-see,

Al - a-bam - a, Al - a-bam - a, We will _ aye be true to thee!

BOOKS

Benoit, Peter. *The Trail of Tears.* Cornerstones of Freedom. Daubury, CT: Children's Press, 2013.

Gosman, Gillian. *Rosa Parks.* Life Stories. New York: PowerKids Press, 2011.

Levinson, Cynthia. *We've Got a Job: The 1963 Birmingham Children's March.* Atlanta, GA: Peachtree Publishers, 2012.

Stille, Darlene. *The Civil War Through Photography.* Documenting U.S. History. Chicago: Heinemann-Raintree, 2013.

WEBSITES

Alabama Department of Archives and History Kids' Page
http://www.archives.state.al.us/kidspage/kids.html

Alabama Symbols, Emblems, and Honors
http://www.alabama.gov/sliverheader/Welcome.do?url=http://archives.alabama.gov/emblems/emblems.html

Official State of Alabama Homepage
http://www.alabama.gov

Official Travel Site of Alabama
www.alabama.travel

Joyce Hart, who was raised in the South, has worked as an educator, an assistant librarian, an editor, and a desktop publisher. She is currently a freelance writer and the author of several books. Her brother-in-law, Dick Ptomey, who grew up in Alabama, can trace his Alabama ancestry back several generations. He had a lot of fun telling Ms. Hart stories about Alabama as she wrote this book.